Shadows
Amongst
the
Threads

J.A. SANTANA

DOWNLOAD THE FREE AUDIOBOOKS!

Grab your FREE audiobooks of
Shadows Amongst the Threads and
The Cool and Warmth of Hearts, narrated by me!

Experience the chilling world of fear and the
passionate realm of love in a whole new way.

JASantana.me/ShadowsHeartsAudio

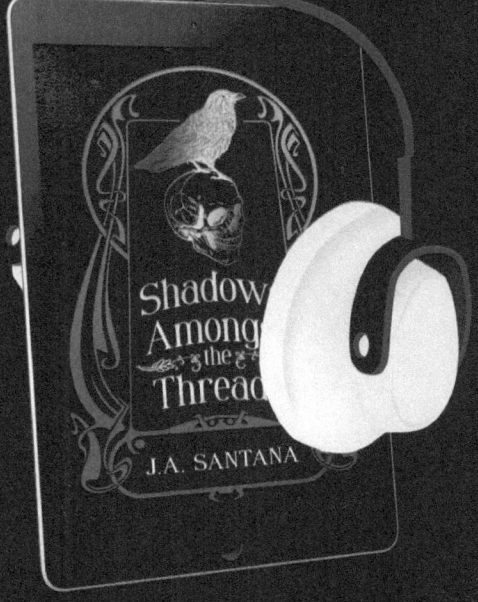

paperback ISBN: 979-8-9854620-4-3
hardcover ISBN: 979-8-9854620-5-0
e-book ISBN: 979-8-9854620-3-6

Library of Congress Control Number: 2022917942

Cover & Typeset Design: *Natalia Junqueira*

Editor: *Michael Martin*

To my family and friends,
and Lady Muse

CONTENTS

Epigraph

"There is no light without shadow and no psychic wholeness without imperfection."

—Carl G. Jung

INTRODUCTION

Shadows Amongst the Threads is a poetry collection of the shadow: the dark side of the personality, comprising primitive, negative human emotions and impulses and the quest for power. Within these pages, I examine the most fundamental fears that inhabit the minds of every one of us. These fears include what lurks in the night, the unknown horrors of disease, malevolence, death, and the suffering of the imagination. Furthermore, I examine the unknowns, the unnatural and unexplained through symbolism - fears and desires (demons), evil twin (doppelgänger), and vanity (Narcissus). We struggle to root out the creative energy posed by our shadow. Of course, certain behaviors and thoughts should be tempered or channeled with proper guidance, so as not to deny the fact they are a distinct part of our nature. We must identify the contents of the shadow and integrate them into our personality. This is the process of "the realization of the shadow", also known as shadow work, coined by Carl G. Jung. Unfortunately, most people are not taught this way. Instead, with the help of culture, we deny ourselves. Whatever we perceive as inferior, evil, or unacceptable becomes part of the shadow. The unexamined parts of our personality do not go away but compound over the years, beginning in childhood, and innate emotions like fear, anger, hate, and shame are allowed to run rampant. This tragedy illustrates how generational teaching continues to polarize emotions. This allows the shadow to surface and manifest itself in some manner. Often, it will begin with a leak of whiplash responses or negative projections but soon transforms into a host of monsters enacting acts of predation, resentment, rage, and malice, all at the cost of false preservation or beliefs. When a culture adopts unfettered hedonism, vanity, or vices, where the unexamined life foments these norms and loses touch with virtues that emulates wisdom for society to thrive with purpose; culture will relegate to the perception of a meaningless and chaotic universe - the unexamined descent into hell. Thus, by not embracing the shadow wisely, then we will never become the wholesome person we need to be, but a hollowed-out husk who wanders nameless, aimless, and shameless about the landscape of obscurity. This poetry collection explores the manifestation of the dark side of our shadows, the monsters born from its depths, not just at the individual level but also in the collective shadow of societies that welcome the encroaching darkness.

And out from the shadow—grew a torrent, a monster, a fiend, the devourer of light, life, and fire; the doppelgänger of thyself.

—J.A. Santana

A Crime Forged in Verse's Rhyme

The sanguine sunrise stirs the calm ocean's waves soon clamor
by sunset and grew the golden wrath stored under one's banner;
a looming silence of despair sank with nightfall embark to tear
the kind gesture and wither control the fog of looming despair.

The odyssey of a sacred song I must venture with haste and there
I sought enjambed verses on broken columns the gloom filling this air
and boiling within the solitude of me—I could not go and bear
the weight of something I unearth and fail to stare
with restless eyes, and what a grave notion of a senseless crime
I remember in the month of December. Oh—quite too severe,
the sea urchins think! An audience of me—was invited here
in the Muses' judgment not mend the dreams that sunder my dear
Euterpe from me for the sin I shall not scribe for this verse's rhyme.

I miss the bliss of it all as I reminisce for a vacant time
in the hope I thought was mine;
In the future I fear was mine
dies the chilled death under bells' chime—
clang and clank and roar with rigor the pall of my time,
while desiring new passions in the mind's gloomy abode;
Athena survey upon me from the knowledge that forebode
a fallen grace in the shadow's depth despite this frigid clime
and time on earth a crime forge in vain for this verse's rhyme.

Alone I

I have not seen of what taunts me—
nor can I unfold what haunts me—
nor what it means! And on this night
something stirs, eludes me—blanked light.
This event bent I—its progress
sought haven to plunder and press
itself further by closing in.
Unknown if I could gain a win
and borrow some strength from within,
and smite away the very sins
that hinder I could not accept
the burdens of lies—I reject.
From this nightfall a heartfelt stain
lingers and this worry remains—
shackle anchored in that corner.
Punished in kind, sought to garner
in the mind's eye—all gone awry,
and believe what I wielded are
idle hands—devil's work did bar—
shackle anchored in that corner,
and shadows of an abhorrent
voice spoil with chatter my torrent
thoughts. A glow exudes at center,
marks a far off place—I whisper:
lowly-form will you take me there?
And it nods and nudges some more
and I stand there from the floor—
never glancing that corner, where
shackles siphon and I lay bare
in its glow, in such eerie form,
a path towards center of storm…

Alone II

Alone in this dearth world I stood,
daily glancing the passersby,
onward vagrants slid past in woods
on nightly watch with heavy sigh—
heavy in gait, sullen in stride.
Hapless souls bare laden with lies—
carried with the weight of what died
in a still motion picture frame—
did not capture the soul of pride;
go about routine all the same,
from windows we rest fearful hands,
and newsmen in their contrived aim,
awash with worry of far lands—
the horror of remote villages—
too soon lost in quickening sands,
while guerrillas sack and pillage,
and such quantitative measure,
a sublime shock burst in spillage,
the woes of unmeasured terror,
a vile nature lurks in the mind
and points outward; and we, bearers
alone in this world, did not find
our glowing path, the very home
of windows unquiet eyes often roam.

An Ounce of Pride

The gain of this night holds an ounce of pride,
sank low chilling tides downpouring the drain.
This night cannot unwind the well of dread,
when she enters; I concoct from a grain
a salve from Gilead help soothe time's
return of voices pouncing my thoughts and slain
a grand desire—playing wildly in haste
in my head, I could not with resolve feign
center of my universe; yet, in pride
the prospect—I fancy with no end fain
me to cherish, as I muse in my head
the mind's crude wishes and choose not in vain
attempt, yield the toil of the poet's rhyme.
Oh—her blissful strides what ungainly reign
in a man's lust and apt reply would raise
an ounce of Alizé—surmount the strain
that hid within an ounce of blemished pride,
and an ounce of her settled pride had slain
these unsettled walls—she tore the threads…
asunder my hollow halls and wild lanes…
crooked where lofty tales with chilling rime
of vacant reach… the wild angst of Spain's
Don Quixote stood his dream a foul taste
sublime by her message… conscript in chains
that tomorrows are written, not what bides
latent lovers but anchors in verses pain
of their harrowing desire in love's red
passion sweeping gently closer in plain
strides—yet the romance of this story's clime
ever filling ounces of pride in quiet rain
were only myths… unsavory in taste
and bore from within what he did not gain.

At a Moments Notice

At a moment's notice, light blankets into darkness;

squelching of a dull breath collapses

the cavernous labyrinths of hollow men and

a glancing blow of humanity loathing existence.

Warmth of skin diminishes in stiff coldness—

putrid aches are cast away and canvases

flesh across nature's bedrock floor.

Death arrives with a promise in its unbridle slur

"Suff'r nuh mor as the duality of bondage wift thee scythe I

shall

releasee thee into the night"

At a moment's notice, nothing left to languish under one's pall

and bear no witness in sight…

Bed of Eulalie

With my passions thy scarlet rot swarms
and unveils Eulalie who once warm
my stubborn soul could not whet;
what the inward mind had not yet
riven upon Eulalie the fair and kind maiden.
And none wiser risen from her that once, laden
with grief, and she nudged with forward eyes
and search afar in listless manners that spies
where thy centered of truth on this first night;
a poet, not scribe, in rhymes, and tresses of golden light
in thy deep cosm of time's unbridle length
where light could not claim in strength
towards my descent in the network of hell;
and oh—Eulalie in kind would salve with her spell.

Stiff roots that spurs the bark of a willow tree,
puzzle by this jester's riddle
and that vile hoary visage marked with trembling
and its foul harrowing piercing screech
and wailing cries heard around these trees;
it could not salve—where Eulalie could not be
and the lifeless husk that haunted the euphony
here and the wordless ghost hovering at my side
fades from me with crooked smile, soon slides
and enters the ageless chilled slumber in the bed of Eulalie.

Cleanse the Sinful Heart

Oh—high heaven cleanse, cleanse the sinful heart;
blacken rot taints the weary rundown soul
on the fortnight eve deep in the north pole
straying further in these deaf willow parts.

In this hostile world, we too soon depart
on the barren road peering for twin souls.
And the dredge of this land bare Charon's toll;
and cleanse the sinful, cleanse the sinful heart.

Glaring eyes gossip amongst shady parts
in their scorn sought valiant deeds that stole
hero's scores and not quell their fervor in toll
straying further in these deaf willow parts.

Ordain by hellish omen, soon depart
innocent's shine in unforsaken souls—
pandemonium reign upon these folks,
and cleanse the sinful, cleanse the sinful heart.

Confined space—whispers discrete in these parts,
a dreadful atmosphere looms in suspense—oh,
from that prison in bedlam could not know
how Van Gogh's Starry Night conveys in art
straying further in these deaf willow parts.

The many fractured dreams of longing hearts,
plagued with misery, in meander stroll
through fallow fields laden with Dead Souls;
shall in time waken heaven and cajole—
and cleanse the sinful, cleanse the sinful heart.

Cutthroat Images

The harrowing haunts on this lone manor,
and sleepless nights filled their walls in bizarre
tongue and veil of spotted dreams in earthstar
lands mid distant oasis in the clamor
of vast dunes of the Mohombi desert—
cannot speak ill of harrowing taboos.
Glisten lucid dreams of the icy girt
in the purview of distant stars that drew
a jewel of crimson—gleam the fervor
of evil's ascension; and bear the wounds
of a man's scorn strained in scars and authors
the salve for these blisters defile these grounds,
and nourish him on his doomed ardent sail;
soon, chapters spiral on its spine and wail.

Dark Foes

Lurkers in the park often remark in the dark.
As they are lurking amid the shadows.
Sheltered in these eerie nights,
desperately stalking a foe,
pondering on a weak soul.
Their boasting,
makes you shiver without sight,
yet, taunting ghosts,
seeking fear in austere souls,
nothing more than vengeance in their howl—
while feeble patrons stumble these grounds,
and the humble may pretend safe passage—
surely, these fiends will feast upon these savages
at the notice of their nervous rumbles;
they are still questioning,
as they loom through the night,
latching from their branch in a threatening glare,
the scoundrels will not pity them for grace—
they have instilled the imagination with plight,
from their grisly cove spying all those in despair,
unaware of their presence, fearing, doubting, and nameless—
under their own demented snare still nameless.

Darkness

I had a night, unlike some other nights.
A nightmare ensnared me of the gone sun,
the star that gave life, its life gone which
left the sights of all with wonder and dread
as the unnoticed stars twinkle what's ahead.
Harrowed the icy chill and the cold earth
Swung around the dim star and with all stars
rove in the darkling without complement.
Morn, noon, eve passed—many were with no day,
and men abstain their passions by the ruin
that sinks low the dread and enters an age
of chaos without light but with the flame
and prayer of this time. Chant that of flame
and the chill that once fills the heart with dread
ignites the watchfire within men, soon bore
the desolate end of thrones. The palaces
of the sunken king, the iron king, the
ivory king; the crowns could not govern
the welfare of nations from their chambers
to their squalors and distant huts outside
the kingdoms' walls—dwell unwelcome passions
flamed the frenzy eyes soon mark the beacons
of burnt cities and awestruck in huddle,
awash by the blazing flame and observes
upon another teeming depth of pain
an angst soon bore to surface and happy
are those on mountain top volcanos: all
was clear in their heartfelt alignment. The
darkness of hope furrows deep and they plunge
with torch ablazing the forest—hours swept
and all that remained the embers of fire
crackling their last breath and with it the last
hope for men and soon fading from sight the
frenzy eye was not extinguished but circle
round the dark soul and this ring of fire clings

tight, an unearthly aspect and flashing
before all—the quietude of the lone night.
And some fell upon knees wailing and some
hung with pale faces and few hurried to and
fro, and fed the dying embers upon
their funeral pyre resolutely—
on the dull sky and it went unconcerned
then swarm a maddening curse toss themselves
upon the dust in their foul flurry gnashed
their teeth and howled deep in the woodland of
weir. In wild flight flapping wing beast daze and
screech in tremor and flutter and frazzle
on the ground; four-legged creatures scatter
about from hounding men and scale hissers
were not safe nor the multitude of legs
that sting—none judge as food satiates hunger.
For a time no banner rose, yet soon it
did and glutton of sin unveil its frown
upon each other; brethren paid in blood
to gorge themselves in sullen gloom and no
love in this and mark the end the age of
scholars. The horsemen of famine swept
with the pang across the lands the vestige
of the entrails of hollowed men; and tombs
amass so glorious a trove of crypts
lined in rows: and this was the apocalypse.
The weak and weary culled and bartered with
tool or clothe; while meager flesh fed upon
meager flesh this pall that fell on the earth.
Wild cats with sunny eyes rustle bushes
as men backstab and pillage lone roamers;
some beast and men conjoin at the hip and
few lucky of this fended and hunted
and the unlucky fell as scraps for the
timid scavengers who cloaked in the veil.
The stilled earth spun and the stars twinkle
and they drift on the black canvas and
two soaring towers leer each other their

might. The land piled in crypts and hollow
skulk warily as sport and the fog filled
a cool warmth and banners flapped in zephyr
gust—and from the silent sabbatical
two imposing factions grew and their eyes
of cinder met besides in crosshair be-
fore the field of dying ember rage, the
raging of arms clash one another as
wave smash in ironclad armor; oh the
unholy things men done onto men of
their own kin: thrust, gnash, pummel, slice, bit, gouge;
and these were not the worst of it as they
ripped hearts, swallowed sight, chewed ears, searing flesh
and famine did not cease their woes—enrage
the frenzied eyes of men. The few bonfires
of dying ember, whimpering flickers
feeble breath, blew into with little life
and held for a time a little flame a
mockery lifted their visage towards
each other visage—saw with shaken sight
the ghastly pale corpse and unbroken stare
flickered flame whimpering in the iris.
With shame moisture seeped and eyelids sank low
and made bed with death's dream kingdom these souls.
The silent sabbatical lived for ages,
the void filled here the might and grandeur snuffed
in the purview of time. The dark star roamed
and the earth—seasonless, herbless, treeless,
manless, lifeless—a quietude for ages went
on the ash lands. And the serene flow of
rivers, falls, and streams slow quietly;
while wind utter silently caresses
the scarce ember abode. The moon hung dark
and still, stirring the tides and the clouds few
they were rarely found round piercing columns;
Darkness's reign with death's twilight kingdom of
empty men dark souls bred the darkling lords.

Days That I Died

Those days that I—I died a thousand deaths
like a wizened child locked in his cradle
when the sustenance of love starved for days
on end with no goodbyes with my last breath.

Rehearse scenes of pride drowning in hell's Lethe
the disdain culture had for my wild youth
on endless film reels cement in replay
Those days that I—I died a thousand deaths.

A hero's call laid unknown ventures ahead
where birds soar towards the sky but the fear
labor the mind of flaws with no praise—say
on end with no goodbyes with my last breath.

Oft—what hides the outworn sword in its sheath
in its dim heart still sings the joys of life
then a torrent swept my hopes to betray
Those days that I—I died a thousand deaths.

And blinding light died with its last faint breath
that night in the warm embrace—dread did slay.
The slayer of my fortune—I abide
on end with no goodbyes with my last breath.

And you, my conscience, in flight with night's tide
shore: never recede and reveal what lay
among those days that I—I died a thousand deaths
on end with no silent goodbyes with my last breath.

Distortions

A splintered wooden cup lingers on the table
with jagged edges, the marks of dead wood.
The peels of the bark of ill-sorrow challenge
the harmony of fading tomorrows, and she

glares on the thin silver moon behind the gauzy gray
clouds; instilling strife that read the lines in doleful
eyes, and wallows that visage onto tear-stain
pillows and hears what bellows in the unquiet heart;

she plucks a rose from its surrounding thorns,
how the encroaching darkness fills over
with a flurry of unrequited love, and
how the service in one's intent stirs the might
of brooding eyes swift to cull the untamed.

Draw in those steps the less able to crawl,
and strive for the longings of novelty. Ashamed
to share what lies in dreams and manifests in reality
and not caress with selfsame unequal solace—
wishing what uttering words could hold from under.

And blaze a torch with Spirit! Or resign
in the landscapes of obscure glens, and the
forgotten wisp of fog lands conceal the dead
eclipse; not enlightened with the rays of the sun
nor cast under the shadow of the moon and hear
the chant of songs soon retreating under the monsoon.

Doppelgänger

Shadow, thy power is to me
like those pallid dark orbs of yore,
that gloomy, o'er a darkened sea,
the fury, way-worn wanderer bore
to his own vacant shore.

On desperate seas long wont to roam,
thy raven hair, thy faceless face,
thy dormant flare, have brought me home
to the glory that was my own,
and the grandeur that was erased.

Lo! In yon brilliant spectral-niche,
how formless-like I see thee stand,
the flame lantern within thy hand!
Ah, Hades, from the regions which
are Unholy-Land!

Dreadfully a Beautiful Plague

The boy often stumbled upon splinter roads ahead, barring
him with wonders of how ample they were from afar;
stood there distraught, contemplating what foul fiend
lived here and felt their menacing eyes that teemed
the might of hell looming unseen in the choking ghastly air.

And, without notice, the acidic burn within it did not spare;
as he sought, a vigorous unease embroiled there of Weir,
swell by the husk of the ash forest, his heart pounded
with the shaken earth, drenched in sweat surrounded
by an unseen grappling of the forest tendrils in Weir.

For too long he wandered in those lifeless woods of Weir.
As it was night full of fright—struck by a looming fear—
he should've never shut his eyes and faced that threat there!
An unwise choice he made in vain, and bent over; he swore
the brittle charcoal road behind was never a scene to adore.

"Oh God," he said, "deliver me from this unbridled pain!"
but could only utter a sigh, wind blaring the unease draining
him and stood a canopy of crooked arms with foul apples.
He sought light in the woods where the sunrays dappled
his safe passage—those grounds did not comply
and ensnared him, unknown what held in this dreadful plague.

His silent shout: "Don't let this plague spread!" netted by its thrall;
he felt it coagulating in his blood—the filth unabated grew a threat
he had never felt: a disease left a smothering icy chill, and as it grew,
he could not discern reality from illusion. Soon to be killed by the
rose's thorn, a silhouette filled over with a crooked stare. And hapless,
in the ghoul-haunted woodland of Weir, that it did not shine on this
dreadful place; yet confounded, why the soot of this rose grew
in these subtle shaded grounds…

Dream

Take this love upon these vows
and ne'er fill the well of what now
are blood stains drowning thy brows;
and too soon rob heaven's gleam
and foment the selfsame dream,
the breed of hate the few say
are the ruins that taint this day.
In the vision I wept the loss
of loved ones in senseless war.
Always miss how I could not cross
where they are and much too far,
the heart not tread to explore
here on surf-tormented shore.
And I hold with center hands
the selfless draw onto sands
of time and expel hope's breath
and bring home my kin from death's
realm; yet in here something creeps!
not of souls themselves, do glow,
and they weep—so they weep!
And what accompanies shall sow
its seed and bear fruit what seems
an unwavering cruel wave
no human can ever save
and I dream within a dream.

Everwinter Nights

Alas—Nyx rides with the cloak of Darkness
the bearer of the night's curses! Keres
fed on men's dread with battlefields as its source,
and all their plight trapped in violent bloody death—
blown to dust and Thanatos drove men to Lethe!

Alas—a lost, lost realm held the last breaths
of roaming soldiers with unclear sight,
oh—the cruel irony festered a blight
on their pledge waning—fomenting their death.

Knights held their knight's honor—in their
stories bound by eternal duty, and it's there
what laid them bound to the kingdom's crown,
where unknown patterns of their shade are known.

Alas—alas! none vengeful spirit shall sway
where no more remembering soul had been
and harmless love was flesh prised from their skin;
nothing but ash of grace in all that lay.

Oh—weary lone heart that no longer mends,
oh—wary lone fear still can't apprehend
where it wants to be, where it needs to be—
in this life—dwell in everwinter nights,
in this life—dwell in everwinter nights.

Fear Bearing Within

The sheer cliffrock of passions I dare not soar with Icarus' wings;
I hid deep in breast much farther than I hope I could not spring,
and deep in this ravine, I have fallen, as I fear it would bring—

the further it goes, the harder I latch onto the rope of hope.
The dark fills and swells all sides common amid tropes,

and the manifold sky gleam what's left upon the cloudless night
and felt the unease of the sublunary tides fomenting a plight

and light not heed my plea and the last of its glimmer call for
safe passage in ashen woods; and the encroaching rumbles bore

the unquiet storm as it circles and casts thee, the tumultuous sea;

never reaching ashore—a creeping fog welcomes a tale of terror
as it hangs on the branch of dead willows and it stirs in error

beneath these grounds and what hid under could not fathom

what the mind told out loud—rested the phantom of lies,
and it bade us muster and draw out the bull; the crimson eyes

must scour what's under and uncover beneath the earth—

in the shadow of shrubs, it said "Do not! Do not! I repeat"
something vicious with its looming gloom stirs it would repeat.

I pursue in haste to unearth what held these harrowing grounds
nestled around in too many mounds, and with what hope I found
that siphons what once bore frightful Erdtree's crooked visage;
and rays could not dapple the husk of these clouds in passage—

mourn how snow will fill these woods all over in frosty torment;
and that uneasy reason, all month's seasons will hastily lament

the songs of strife their requiem, mourn the loss of life its sound
and with sins charge on that upward climb to the hilltop mound;

forlorn a ravage sea and hangs the blood moon above the fold
and the shapeless clouds obscure the night sky foretold

lands between within a fear bearing within,
and the pocket of hope I have stored within,

not bear the fear within its hope.

Glutton of Decadence

The culling—too soon comes in strides! And from under
nothing on this earth has shown the pain we labor in vain.
Austere souls circle and circle without word, and worries
rolled up under hefty sleeves are enough to haunt folks
of these gated streets; alas, deceived and promised;
perhaps, believed and tarnished. The quarrels of life
are not handed upon the dead—engrossed in ghastly
scenes in The Second Coming—hardly deserves
seven thousand lashes. Peer over the horizon search
for Sisyphus's unending toil: an undercurrent will reveal
the imprint of the coming Revelation at hand
and surely not end with just The Third Coming!
And do not judge the thrall of crowds with dismay
nor provoke unkindly for the selfish charity of the masses;
the hypocrisy of our times are buried in the spirit
of distant heroic deeds that no longer confront
the simulacrum villains of self-aggrandizement
seeking fame at the cost of the *Spiritus Mundi;*
as the peacock puffed up its ornamental feathers
while the uncommon crane soared towards the sky.
A decaying society could hardly own its shadow—
and bury deep these confessions on broken pillars
of tribute and the gild in the eyes could only goad
the voice of a mad mind; the voice of an unfettered mind.
What harm is worth a fool's errand, whose ephemeral indulgence
faintly stirs and all too common the Will to Power grows heavy
And heaven congregates to save these souls from shifting winds,
And has a little more of the burnish fire and heaven's gleam
cast over and the shadow seeks closure with the Spindle of Necessity.

Illuminate a Path

The flesh-devouring Cerberus fed
upon the dying souls where they fled
to Hades gates soon met the last shout,
"Illuminate a path," before their end.

Odin's ravens of darkness descends
where dull eyes often hither unseen—
the tarnished human soul had not been:
not gleam to illuminate a path.

Anubis swarmed like a desert storm to scathe
for the deserted in these scorch scarring sands;
Fates saved their journey into the hinterlands
and eerie foul things live in these wooden lands
of Pan and they kept close a lantern at hand—
Illuminate a path or nightmares shall swallow

with what slender hope is gained—shall follow
if woes lie in these uneven meadows
and trek through the uneven bedding
with forward eyes nor towards feeding
abode in dense shrubs where creeping
eyes stirs one's soul in fright—pleading,
"Illuminate a path… illuminate a path."

Immortal

Psyche, I grow tired being locked here,
suppressed by all those childish fears;
and you have not welcomed me here;
and dared not tread to meet near
where our presence lingers long here,
A burden soon racks you with shame!

These wounds won't seem to leave,
this pain transmuting the grief
that harrows a horror on the eve
with the crimson rage shall receive
thee; the weight of disdain shall achieve
the rapture of my love revealed in name!

At once then the unbent time of thy light
bound us to no end; the conjoin might
tremble the outward forces; bedight
their firstborn the norms they smite,
I in thy deep chamber only benighted
an unkempt fervor one day sharing its fame!

And your nights of unpleasant dreams
shall soon open the gate and teem
with the collective wit, shall stream
an unfettered darkness, the extreme
of which bore the death of thy gleam
and shall whimper—the end of thy flame.

In These Walls

In these walls, dark figures speak faintly

not in usual tongues

the pounding of rain against the window they shriek loudly—

chanting! So these walls do not give weight to what closely

kept these aberrations enclosed in their domain.

Terrified by the prospect as they surround all four nooks—

why the floor suddenly creeks!

Have they altered space ever so fervently

with a ghastly aim in mind?

Unable to budge where I laid anchored in the spook-

iest of fright, I scour for matches to light the furnace

before the whisperers of darkness are able to find

a life of vigor an enticing a meal for such fiends to devour

in haste.

And the harrowing scene did not bode well in earnest

here in these walls. This shall be my fate

and hate peering what hid in these walls before it's too late.

Inside Vacant

Unending thirst has taken its firm hold
and this sinking dread burrows deep in folds—
and torture like a film reeled its last tape.
In her siren, she crashes, shores up, and drapes
shipwrecked sailors and the sight of terror
amid an unbroken chain fill with horror
in earnest favor towards maiden's plea,
Oh, how ignorant I have grown to be
enthralled by a thirst—an urge I comply;
no favor gained in restraint—only wry
the mind! What horrid form reeked of peril—
I choose not in care and, ceding her thrall,
I seek in prayer, forbidding such displeasure.
Yet, enough spooking me by its sheer measure
and for its sprouting in the next hour—hour
of ghastly horror—I pluck my eyebrows,
I hope to curb—curb this bestial power.
In fear, I came undone, unknowing how.

Invisible Affliction

I have sought the pain that wrought me, and night
was no less kind aiding me, as the rain
pummeled my way down the freeway—the plight

here of muted sky tremble on this lane;
as clouds stood unpassed—unfurl the wool
of an invisible wound—and it pains

the mind of wonders; eerily dreadful
as much, and I jest to what laid in these
somber recesses that irk unforgetful

climes hanging at the forefront: where it freezes
fervently on the discomfort that hangs
and burrows itself with horrid unease—

to what end does the worst kind of affliction
self-inflict the bane of my invisible existence?

Lady of Sorrows

The wretched despair brought upon it:
Lady of Sorrows in that was transparent
and she sets the crumbs on this path, that wrenches
lovers' and clutches them under a miasma of decay!
An acrid odor that filled an unsavory taste
lamenting ad nauseum soon ripped apart—
the unending gloom of sorrows;
oh—the ghastly unseeming horror
of heightened senses makes this part
hard to bear; and the cracks in these walls
foreshadow the arid sting in my nostrils;
and in her chateau a chilling winter's austral
wind blisters a bacterium that looms the halls.
Oh—the deafening choke of miasma swarms
and maggots crawl with a forewarn sickness,
swirling around and driving to the ends of earth a madness
authored by the cruel maiden, the sufferer of my sorrows
that brought upon an agony of unending tomorrows.

Let It Burn

When the wind frays against a bitter fool.

It came to an end when worn pages blew in the wind,
when shadows grew thin;
when memories strayed from hearts.

Scorn feelings drift, the timid body grows weary,
the mind clogs in confusion.

Don't let this feeling go,
don't let it end without a sensible solution,
nor want the memories to linger on endlessly alone,

and bear the guilt that regrets outlive
and with golden chariots steer us to forgive
and cement how one is to live.

It came to an end when worn pages blew in the wind,
and the shadow grew thin,
memories would stray from beneath the skin.

Scorn feelings drift, timid souls grows weary:
the mind bottled in turmoil.

Don't let this feeling go,
don't let it end without a sensible resolution,
nor want the memories to linger on endlessly alone,

and with great floods the ills of harvest,
What good comes in bad company;
when unlocked doors to furthest
Towers crumble under uncomfortably.

It came to an end when worn pages blew in the wind,
when wrinkles on aging faces feel
the fading memories on its last reel.

Scorn feelings drift, timid souls grows weary,
the mind bursts with illusions.

Don't let this feeling go,
don't let it end without a sensible proposition,
nor want the memories to linger on endlessly alone.

Scorn feelings are often so appealing—
are we so evil that we kindle this upheaval?
Espy an oasis blurred in the desert sands,
and rub the sight of doubt to grasp these grains of sand.

It came to an end when worn pages blew in the wind,
when shadows grew thin;
when memories stray from hearts.

Scorn feelings drift, the timid body grows weary,
the mind clogs in confusion for all eternity.

Don't let this feeling go,
don't let it end without a sensible solution,
nor want the memories to linger on endlessly alone.

When the wind frays against a bitter fool
is it for the good: the change we need to cradle resolve?
Or turn a blind eye and bid farewell never return to absolve
the scars and let it burn harshly for life-clinging fools.

Life Taken of Fire

Life unseen, blessings die unseen;
passions filled with wild pleasures
bear in them intricate messages—
and demons confine this nature.

Life's principles we seek in heart—
and one's desire longs for fire
in one's temperament: measure
by the Patron Will of Justice.
In the bleakness of days, nothing
gold can stay; at least forestall
the Tempest of Time—cruel Tempest.
Oh—the sign of wisdom within
quiet souls bestow by heaven's fruit
and all drifts under the slumber
with stilled memories laid too soon.

Lilith

I feared the worst while not suspecting this loss to be the loss.
Torn apart as fissures opened its gaping mouth from the moss;
unknown ahead. If I trod further in the monster's nasty jaw,
where the demon lashed out in the untempered manner by claw,
and felt the seduction in her devilish eyes that soon would crumble
my resolve, and I would have bargained against the trembling
of this pact as long as her hand shall not clasp its clasp—
onto men of sailors hooked in the torrent of the demon's grasp;
And she cradled my wildest dream, a crimson of desire that rasped
the demon's joy and rang discord of my ire. And she swore
an oath that echoed with chills the unease I should not adore.
The wailing that pounded these shorelines bolstered a cry,
shedding enough tears and dotting each star in the night sky.

And in the fallen silence where jagged stone creaked
and blood seethed around her teeth and the demon spoke!
    "Fools, give way too soon, lost in a woman's glimmer."
In my bated breath reply,
    "It's in our fallen nature: what heaven fastens for sinners."
"Lips swift to cull." her reply.

I heard the demon's last words while my eyelids sank,
and it said "sleep" in an unearthly tone as it deeply sank

and, cast under her spell, she saunter in the chasm of hell
and months go by without pause as watchful eyes foretell
all at the scene of his demise with the headline that reads:
    "The fate woven in this man's thread'."

Lonesome

Take me away… from this vile domain
to a far-off place where my mind shall lay.
Make me stay… free from this gruesome pain
by fading stars and find a place to lay
in jest from a falling, trembling sky.

The outward window ice crackles
and fogs crawl with ghostlike shackles
and rode upon the city—Tower of Babel
in the hubris with a maddening rattle
swept abroad by heaven's gold wrath.

Take me away… from this vile domain
to a far-off place where my mind shall lay.
Make me stay… free from this gruesome pain
by fading stars and find a place to lay
in jest from a falling quivering sky.

Scorn that I am, forbid this shadow,
unfurl the black wings of the carrion crow
to reincarnate and venerate all my woes
and ascend with this verse's rhyme
to rid my crimes what I will do in time
and request for lonesome forgiveness.

Set me free, free from the bonds of sins,
set me free of this lonesome dreadfulness.

Metamorphosis

My tepid scorn upon all that loved and they
withered until nothing left but wisps' whispers
as I love myself and fail to command what I
love to miss as Narcissus did with all splendid life.

Toiling much the stock of my labor, and they shall
ingress upon the soul's blackened iris
and bear witness the stage fright of my laments,
and trample the ego so deep an error I've spent.

In the deep roots of that malleable center
lay the unflame huntsman and the coveted hunt
never the twain shall meet... so I pine, and
extend my lips upon that mirror lamenter.

Summon from Pandora's box the last of hope
imparting with Aion's favor, a nimble mind
unfolds the answer it seeks and sustains the tremors
of his vain heart—a carousel fomenting his warcry,
and bear witness Narcissus metamorphosis:
winter snow petals surrounding a sunglow heart.

Moon Dimmed From Sight

I wandered lonely on the dimmest night,
unsaid voices that once held a sacred oath
of untold secrets chant in hollow walls.
And the romance of stars of unfounded
pain were of myths, and a growing disdain
filled the inward eye—warped by Grim himself
and claimed by darkness, strife, and tossed
into the obscure sea where ocean's foam
rumbled the depths that held devil's grim visage
and died that night as the moon dimmed from sight.

And the unkindness did not salve the harm felt
and further swarmed the last charm that it held:
a hospice of dreams—the well of last hope
turned passive folks towards cruel beggars;
and the grisly torrent that streams in curves
and swells the ire of watchers swept up
in their fury and impaired by Grim's scythe
and made inquiries of shackle men, sank
unhurried and took from them their light,
and died that night as the moon dimmed from sight.

And this evil robbed the light of joys and
these treasured scenes smashed under labor's fist;
and shimmers ripple on moonlit starless nights
and bear the ash with the fall of lotus flowers,
sour eyes clenched tight with the bluster of zephyr
and died that night as the moon dimmed from sight.

And darkness fills all seasons and marked souls
soon hollow in trembles scathed by harsh winds
and died that night as the moon dimmed from sight.

The presence amid here that shadows fill,
hardly stood quite near as time's keeper shrill,
with its foul scourge and suffused in darkness
and burrowed deeper to weaken this hearth
and the accursed tarnish once shine with gleam
soon died that night as the moon dimmed from sight.

Ode to Thy Dull Blade

I

Life, "The Great Scourge" in that nether twist,
prevailing with the strife pouring poisonous wine
and "The Great Sufferer" on thy pale forehead it kiss'd:
thy immoral acts shall descend upon Proserpine's
scales and weigh on thy soul and punish with yew-berries;
and thy hubris, thinking of quiet shame, death shall be
as nails in notches and splinter thee, foul
ghosts nested in the shadow, yet, we welcome them
in dreams, woven in all seams of nightmares how
tales of the romantic past help feign the sight of them
as they glisten on these threads, and beg to sew these threads
into patches for our cold unkempt beds.

II

The shadows of past could not contrast thy fall
of present shadows: this very thing that fills us with fright
and under the moonlight gleam shall
normally ease is wrought in insomniac nights
of distorted dreams formulated in the ashen hollows sought
in fantasy—in this world of unrestrained hedonism—buds within
a maelstrom ever and ever extending its reach to consume
the treasures of our humanity. Blindness towards fleeting scenes
we gladly take upon with brooding eyes—unseeing wonders,
dimming of spirit that swiftly runs down and doom
by the rote acts of mindless wandering; the myriad of golden
handcuffs, the promise of a dream, the shackles beholden,
the pursuit of unhappiness; as a weeping cloud
fosters a reply that unknown ventures common falls
brand a message to wear our failures in fear: a shroud
where not even the ills of nakedness could pierce and stall
the dull blade. Yet, turning tongue in cheek summoned,
a deep well where many monsters lurk and invites them
with open doors to secure themselves too soon a home.

III

And the sunrise arrived and soon met with dusk in those hours
with the swing of Death's scythe—and offer us the song
of reprieve for the insufferable existence where it waves
thriving in the tumultuous nature of sorrows and rose
again the next day, hid in those final scenes told in epic rave
of warriors within all—while, the tormented mind in the throes
of pangs of anguish brought upon every day by society's unending
shackles; we possess a power to tame thy wild fiction
that scours too deeply; thus surely we must cajole and bring
the well of hope and dispel the nightmares of such affliction
in support of humanity. Instead, imprison by Ephemeral's soft hands
jolts the Psyche a deep, deep itch in thy brow shalt hereby
hound us towards end of earth as we ruminate, and solemnly swear
in oath drawing back the devil's pact and chosen not to bore life's toolkit;
where we sharpen our blade and work with technique, and with this tool
we can bear any storm and journey with shadow or wander amidst
the lukewarm moss with a dull blade.

Ode to Thy Dying Day

I

Sunder us in two! Bear not the upshot
of that foul dual nature; and see with human eyes
what bores these tearful falls—wrought
an angst underneath these waterfalls are fair cries
tearing a rift at unmet times. No longer distinguish
the conduct from the task of the mistress shade
upon her smokey lips. Father Time, I ask in favor,
in swift relief gently tip the hourglass and each
grain of sand laid in it an anguish filled in lies;
furnished by an evil fiend with unrestrained malevolence
metastasizing the lies of the demons in my view
who goes forth in cruel manners and robs us
of that divine nature. And the meaninglessness of false psalms
perpetuate the lies fortifying our menial days.

II

Oh—hail *Monday* with its blade lunged into the heart, enthralling in
tears pent-up rage; impounding the lonely beating heart
and in haste of every passing second, minute, hour,
and day. Oh—the lonely beating heart bleeds—
what power produced by this grotesque scene!
Have we not in conviction pled in compassion for our fallible state?
What remains is a grim tale: we were not formed from a smooth slate.
And the affliction dances upon us infectious—spore and traverse all limbs
give rise to the overcast of our shadows bearing their grudge.

III

Bleeding *Tuesday* has arrived! Let us rejoice! Mark this day
on Earth's stone tablets; and not be coy by its pinch of strife.
A key measure that allots the golden years of life
where joys once held the luxury of laughter—and *Tuesday*
has plucked from brow and the weight of these blocks stuffed

in invisible bags we fill in shame. And with *Tuesday* thrust,
a faint scene seeps to the surface rallying to take back the bread of life:
from which, daily tolls wear down the soul by the rust
of unsharpened tools. The omen has come to pass on bloodshed to feed,
deep upon its rage and bear its grudge the fall
as it hovers within sight in cheeky expression, treads
undignified in stern erection bearing its dark energy upon all!

IV

In the midst of *Wednesday*, we celebrate all day long
in the vast joys of the closing week. A renewed sense
returns the steadfast battering of tides, while we pine for their loss.
Here we are carved by yesterday's storms, conflating today's hope.
    Are we not in further reach?
    —elapse *Thursday* through *Friday*,
all the same weals and woes; scattered sweat stains,
    and curdling blood strains—
laid upon the scarring wasteland of bubbling froths. Today,
have… we settled upon *Saturday* and too soon sprung *Sunday*,
a river of no end?—One can only know what horrors these broken fields
of battered shields and nicked swords strewn here around
    like landmines. What betrays these grounds—
prophesied lies, lost in gossip—words unable to save; and here
they furrow in these poor souls beneath thousands of mounds unknown.

V

Monday through *Sunday* has come and pass
as all before them, and with their last eulogy raise a glass
in honor of menial labor; their days were numbered, alas.

Of Dark and Flame

I

In the Age of Dark of ashen lands, fashion the still mild husk the sufferings of mortality. And for epochs, many there were of dusk in dank caves that few knew the quiet stillness that the gods and goddesses hold in tale steering the fate of humanity. Out from nowhere in Lethe befell the spark of flame, the bearer of heat and cold, death and life, and romance of light and dark in their constant old dance—a Titan held the pity of their frail flesh. And moths to a flame—wanderers from the shadow grew a lust for that scintillating flame and bearing this gift ensued heaven's rage. Heaven judged upon him a silent suffering: intense it was for all time. And betrayer of his kinship without fail marks the end of the Age of Dark, inviting the Age of Fire birthing thriving gilded nations with renown felt by heavenly lyres. Eons pass of grandeur until the flame's first whimper portends the gradual fading of nations' descent towards the perpetual bleakness, unwelcome encroachment of darkness. These myriad souls cling tight to all their possessions and swarm a veil unlifted as grain of sands howls from Zephyr's wind. And flames ember in their lowly strain, muddle cry shall surface a mindless madness as they only saw not fading light but of the looming endless nights. And the vigil of unsung heroes bearing the dark sigil and majestic lush lands began losing their luster and ever-growing upon it flush the hands an ashen tinge and unsung heroes set forth venturing unhinge northward in the harsh, frigid north toward heaven's pole, a firmament betwixt them, and beheld the crimson visage of gods and the cosmic serpent spun while laden in ascent awaiting the end of days and this is their fate heaven forestalls.

II

And long from that slumber in the frigid north awakened by a dream within a dream of a murky, forgotten, forsaken land, a place of which souls salve ailing minds met an augur of darkness for it all to be lost from an unknown brand, a curse of sorts the symbol the lone Titan suffering flesh it marks. And none worse without meaning and this fleeting notion of demeaning will not matter as ephemeral flesh morphs into a being of frenzied eyes and unceasing heaven in deaf tyranny welcomes this fate, ruling long a disdain. And they will be awakened and stirred from their ailing dream that once gilded nations walled off far from them, driving them towards a venture in haste the all seeming familiar poles, they barely grasp in language and learn of its dilapidated state at the high wall gates! And this demarcation refused mortals from seeing the grand stage of life, but eternally embitter their seething unsated thirst as it steers them forward toward a multitude of doors; time shall reveal this fate while thunder wrung, and flung between divine and worm racked with this torment and the Titan in daily anguish of heaven's judgment looks upon the weals and woes of mortals in their silent sentence and passing seasons exude the golden scales, judge upon heaven's vain repentance, and from this vain guilt share in consonance with the dark.

III

And unkind time, the estranged time merges upon the mountain of kingdoms crumbled under time's clasp and every kingdom divided against itself, smeared in blood, death, and decay of yore; the Titan unforeseen this human tragedy and he thought in kindness, meant to salve the sum of human wretchedness and strengthen their minds—a tinge in time; yet, above all this converged many lords—all lords destined and merged by the estranged passage with the flame of posterity. And this truth known, known by pilgrims who sought only to find empty thrones and fading flame—the enduring spirit prized from heaven the Titan installed upon human and human vanity with woolen eyes the symbol and sign instilled in mortals their fate and force! And heaven tremble at this and toll the bell emboldening the flame! And as with flesh dusting onto earth tolling bells rang louder and waken men's flame from their dire deep slumber and these vagrants in their newfound course wander further from their thrones and the unsung hero of yore, the nameless wide-eyed mortal—a dimmed shadow of godlike power is compelled as ash seeketh embers is fated to unravel unhindered where no path leads and unbeknownst to them awaits yet compelled to seek it insatiably! In the whit of time, the pall clothed over men's eyes forgets in meaning and soon returneth to their ancient cave. Such is fate... if flame should outlive its selfish gain and invite the dark to reign in equal strides as it denied the natural cycle its date.

Rain I

Pouring down the mask of stained shorelines,
illuminates the debris flowing down the Rhine
brought onto mortals where no other lifeform
on Earth could ever wreak with such art form;
the hidden historical sea of blood filling Earth
and shame the red planet Mars its worth.

Allow the golden rays to mend the hero's warcry
to save within the saint before the rain enslaves him to his primitive cry
and this blissful soldier awaits a fate that soon descries
on the folds of scorched battlefields in the coming of May's
blossom by a rose's kiss and its thorn tore through his armor and slays
the critters that surround his heavy heart with love's allay.

Yet, the presence of a soul disembodied from this life,
churns the eternal strife by the vain wrath that rives
under the arrows of Cupid's scorn, and it pours down a rain
high on ravines where eagles soar and lion's roar reigns
with power that stirs sleeping ghosts from their den,
pouring down without rest hiding humanity's sins:
never shall the shoreline recede therein;
never reveal the tainted blood in these depths;
never misplace the inscription scribed of history's pain,
from which we silently lock under the pouring rain.

Rain II

When the rain fell from high above;
the pain trembled on heaven's love.
Seasons of time, lone a dim view;
held false crime and this truth it knew
how raindrops, drips in loneliness,
sustain drops wail the coziness
of yester warmth; and rain mocks the way tears fall,
and heaven's love bears Grim's atmosphere for us all.

Rain III

Rain falling from high above,
Underneath it all is heaven's love.
Cloudy skies, cloudy skies, smudges hung.
Oh—rainy sky pouring down men's twisted tongues.
Why it cannot be said the same with doves,
flew over high these skies with heaven's love.
Oh—rain drops, drips in loneliness,
people are confused and merciless.
Rain mocks the grieving tears and gloom is quite near;
let those tears mimic the dew that hangs on leaves,
a shallow scene—soon gone it shall leave!
Hear it cascade in the throng of the blackened cave;
hear the plops of water drops hidden in this dank cave,
dormant as they bounce the bed floor, evermore
plops of water drops hidden in this dark cave,
a shallow scene—soon shall it pour
dormant as they bounce the bed floor, evermore.

Restless Nights

Restless nights have taken their toll
on a toilsome body that wants to extol
the flame searing the fatigue she stole,
and the restless nights that seemed to know.

And promised not revisiting her captivating spell
that shackled my senses I could not tell;
and the shame that fell upon her witch's enchantment;
I could not resist her deathly lady enhancement.

My sight grows weary with each passing restless night,
shuddering to keep them stretched apart and worried nights
shall bear trouble with my peers with a heavy plight.

On those restless nights, lucid by that first lull
as she sauntered closer, my senses dulled,
in my obscure aim—glimpse upon her rose
cheeks and the sparkle in her eyes know
no hostility. And I sank with no aid but struck in awe
what she had instilled was worse than I could have foresaw.

I clasp under the weight of that horrid scene—the disdainful cost
of so many restless nights and an image of her red embossed
satin dress dissolved my iron gate and frost on my senses
with vivid scenes of her tempestuous hold on my expenses.

Rust Webbed in Golden Crowns

Oh, how the concealed chasm of the mind,
too often sailing in a sea of thoughts,
yet how deep and webbed, we must scour to find.
In the chasm of such place, held a plot
of land and reap from this soiled earth the dream
of desires hidden from hand and seize
in truth could not sync in heart and what seems
buzzing in the mind laid in cryptic keys
of doors barred by gold gates of light's divine
figures. We did not heed the unseen climes
of unforeseen fate—bramble in stiff vines.
The concealed edges that are strangely sublime,
stemmed the dark roots of one's beloved succor,
a majestic crown hidden in gestures.

Sensible Quite Ignorant

In the cruel curving world that told lies
And ripples with many dark ecstasies

the vain youth entering here is not welcome at all.
How sensible we think we are until our first fall;
soon depart onto ventures with eager fruit
and soon return as turmoil of ventures gives root
of that vain youth. We cease to act sensibly
and the untamed benighted with scarcity by authority
and scattered by zephyr's gust and I wonder why, I worry.

The indignation of indecision jerks its ugly head
and doubt swarms the fragile mind—*dare not tread*—
and by this revelation a complaint stirs a truth;
and I shiver by this audacious assertion of the vain youth.
Then an inner voice whispers *Dare not pass this threshold
or in your chosen gamble you shall reap what is foretold.*

Yet, I hear that low growl curbing desires the heart wants
and seek the truth of my vain youth, inpatient enough,
and sense what naturally fills with roving minds but haunts
the prudence that sensible manners could not comfort the stuff
that sang the vain nature in our ambivalent heart.

When this truth unravels and retentions are met,
I'll be in the grand service of that Will that wishes to bet
that the story of my book will come to a close
and preamble the world his rests in the world he knows.

Serenade Amongst the Dusk

The sheer solace light stretches beyond domains;
soon, hastening night unveils chaos all the same,
and strays when the lone heart could not arraign
the passion sought and dissolves a frail frame.
When fear fills its shadow on this steep climb;
lanterns not alight souls their wayward home
and lost in these eerie grounds a verse's rhyme
in velvet purple could not soothe what fiend roams
these harrowing grounds. A wise man once said,
"An old man's regret is an old man's hell,"
adding in jest, "What regret isn't one's dread?"
Bestowed by heaven's favor, in grief, I dwell
and serenade under the still moonlight,
castaway as a memoir of hope's light.

Serendip

An ash tinge engulfed upon a lone world:
clouded under these gloomy skies, a knife
held the end of time, and the afterworld
befell with the night sky of clasping strife.
And pouring in a deluge, sprawling
shadows of hollow men will come of age
and Death awaits as it lays and hauling
mankind to its breast and urged the gilded grace
of a nymph from her shores and played from her
lyre help bear from the dark brand of chains
and rear an heir free from opaque skies and stir
the binds of scarlet rot that plagues the soul
and bear the discontent of this world's ego
and the bearer of all this ash tinge is slain.

Shadows Trailing Amidst the Ash Nights

The Father of the Abyss projects an immeasurable tide
sweeps beneath the crowd as it looms an unmeasurable stride;
and the creeping phantom that feeds upon weary folks coalesces
itself in the dark and these petrified folks ensnared in pale fear,
unable to squiggle their way out of this horrid dread as it nears
the abyss of horror, awaits the fate of their plight—the unblessed.

The hubris of these sad souls redress their will in prudence;
and diminishes the Holy Grail steering towards what fell near;
and this looming shadow, fed in journey's chasm out here,
and these ashen souls held their lunacy abreast the malevolence
through the darkened path, and they choke off this thin foul air
and wander aimless amongst ghouls and ghosts of Weir.

The blood curdles and metastasizes a sore; and its comfort
changes course, vacillates anguish in fervent discomfort;
this swirling void swallows hope and soon parted the innocence
of heaven's shine and it tapers the inward mind of humankind;
it hinders the mending heart and pulses waning dissonance,
swept in the shadow and sings the silent requiem of the unkind.

The hollow shadow swallows its last will of light
and ripening darkness,
the specter of unhope; its last plea under moonlight,
"Save us from darkness,
it urges these souls as shadows trailing amidst the ash nights."

Shallow

From that sweet nectar in Eden where divine stood
held close the Tree of Knowledge and had
souls not ate of that fruit riddled with falsehood

would not have left them in agonize shame; with that clad
in garments and guided by seraphs out the gate and this
herald the age of darkness… and the requiem sung of sad

souls scoured in shrouds with the ashen kiss
and twenty more scores of this and this bind
bound by these facts the act of which pits

wherever trampled souls tread. The wind
ferments with its abrasive gust
… and scratches in these tormented minds.

Strength could not lend against a ghostlike foe.
Patience could not bear the only hope
on light's broken column, nor stir unhopeful souls.

And it whispered from Pandora's box, "hope…
the best and last of all things and without hope
time pushes and forces all outward like a centrifuge

nudges with a madness frozen in limbo from refuge."
Hollowed vagrants roaming in the lightless dark
of these halls, where pillars of light once pierced the dark,
are fears that fill the hollowed-out husk with no flame spark.

Tale of a Sleeper's Mind

At midnight, in the month of June,
first sin stagnates under the moon.
Could not illuminate the dim,
oral exhale of that golden rim,
nor prize in light of wisdom drop
that centers hand on mountain top,
and lantern carried drowsily
and tread across a steep valley
in ashen lands of sophist grave,
pain sustain a trembling wave;
a passion wrapped with equal strides
and it conjoins at the hip side
and sways the dense fog on thy breast
and passion ruins on thy rest!
Look, Mary—see with straight eyes the lake,
an unconscious slumber would take
and fear would leave this world awake.
No beauty sleeps! And lo! where lies
thy burden of wisdom resides!

They shrill "Were it not better done!"—
a hollow cliche echoed the din,
swift in offer rarely hearkened;
and with raised glass peer the horrors,
and the toils of shame unveil the error
of hypocrisy! And splendid
moments not apprise the blended
lies! In their lack of foresight
not veil the vanity from sight.

The manifest harm of language
and grand fortune could not sandwich
in equal parts—yield the rot of
bad harvest and a shadow shoves

a plague that sweeps across the masses,
welcomes an unkind gift passing
through the shaken mind—unquiet deep
stir in error the fault that sweeps!

It burrows deep in the distant sleep
a chamber of something that creeps
moralists to their knees and hell
is this place of a cruel witch's spell
spurred in madness of melancholy
of one's plight not paint the holy
safety in any strokes of ideals;
ideals brushstrokes dare not heal.

And the many blank canvases
stood quietly here and the damndest
shamefully not raise their mirror
a resonance that in error
not of higher order in them;
could not drum a common well from
resolve the tormented shores of
Ego's door that stretches and soon shoves
tales of a sleeper's mind concealed
the far and many ugly truths
that would drift without heaven's clues
in the chasm of hell looming with wraiths
of one's untamed desires soon lost in faith.

The Burden of Hope

It shot through the night sky a fading star
and they seized a glimpse of this omen's message
that dreamt the descending angel, whose passage
cradled few hearts with a mighty lance and smear
men with fear and fed all their loneliness
expelling light and impelling darkness.
Sins soon return, and tearing down their hopes;
and these weary souls still cling to the tropes
that crawl with a troubling angst she produced
and clash to cope soon lost in her amuse.
The burden of hope shall fade in the mist
as their fervent prayers were their wrong-
ful sin and held her blade and cross the mist
of tragedies famous in this verse's song.

The Craven

I

Once upon a night, a melody plays scarcely in these lonesome days, beholding the unsteady scales; tragically in this tale—foretold in a dream a sight unseen nor skin to squeeze nor sound to squeak nor smell the foul air I wish to breathe as I hid beside this ghoulish tree and I flee before they tear me to pieces— yes this and only this—
   nothing more to see.

From that weary scene, I contemplated in reason I feared that stood near to heart as treason; mourning in awe as it occurs: *how oft do you pine my name in the same way as emotion stirs?* The absence makes fondest thoughts of thee grow strongest. Curiously, a forgotten phrase seems quaint, and its measly taint swiftly rotten my lovely saint—
   merely this and nothing more.

Unkind Time making haste, and choosing not to mind. O Time—hear my sickly plea drown those sordid scenes in the deep dark dreary sea—frowning such request imparts no sight of thee and reminiscing the first kiss filled in glee, and departing this world by *Its* cruel scythe; as it should be—it should be I'm sure the foul fiend will unmake me—
   yet, *Its* door *It* will not pass and nothing more.

My soul grew weaker, shackled by "truth" she no longer sang, "Love." I seek fro' her—soothe my wonders and wandering amid hollow grounds element'd flesh from soul; what hellhole these grounds not gently napping, abruptly rapping inward-minds, not in kind—resigning quietly in the night, sadly fervor these souls their might!—
   more than ever and nothing more.

Deep in darkness weeping, creeping in bushes, in trees, foraging weak and weary of those who squeak! Nor sneak unsound in silent unbroken, unbridled wisp roaming, nor risk as its token. Impetus of night lisp thy name wondering, fearing, doubting, peering far from prayer; not harken my plea and vindication of sins, if this should be
   "yes," echo murmur—"yes, this and nothing more."

Alas—inward-mind! Chamber doors burning trails and turning as I scour repeated halls; halls of mirrored unending lines, disjointed surely— designed by something undivine and winds shifting, changing and misguiding! "Eventually," said I, "eventually, these walls echo close to mark; then I shall see the mystery that eludes me, no more!"

A mystery I finally explore—the one I called Lenore!

II

Unwavered night: I wandered lonely still in the dark, dark, dreary vacant lot, I'm disturbed what sought here—disturbed by what peerless lurkers forebode here; as my body hair bristled while wild cats with their sunny eyes fixed their gaze upon my soft flesh rustled in bushes and ravens stoic with their death stare upon my blacken iris—

this I feared most, nothing more!

The howl of this frightful night, clasped by Terror, subdued by *Its* voice; spooked on this eerie gloomy night, creeping midnight hour, nearing the sneering of watchful eyes; kept peering, rustling in shadows, snapping twigs and dead leaves, tapping bark of trees with menacing eyes scheming in a crowd wishing I—a thousand deaths in one gasp of breath—

evermore and nothing more.

I summon the arms of stoic heroics, channeling courage, combating night's terror; alone in our fancy we suffer more horror than ails the sting of bloody thorns to one's many phobias; a rotted mind: worsens and worsens, foul nature and her aberrations of the night that haunts—she beckons satyrs in desecrated lot and they sought, I—

this I'm sure and much more.

The mist grew much hazer and voices grew much louder, grating eardrums, and succumbing twisting tongues! How can I subside the voices of this monologue? I've sought balm from the unearthly soil ameliorating these taunts, bearing within each day, bearing within each night; bearing within each stay, bearing within each plight—

"'Tis all this and nothing more!"

I'd tried comforting, long philosophical walks, to mull over the voices that stalks; the haze thickened and nothing harkened my plea; while night darkened. The pain grows feverish, my lady's form grows devilish. I scan for answers and too soon invoke ghouls and ghosts who provoke troubled minds; as they harken, bidding me and my

love, adieu—"'Tis this and nothing more!"

Heed my prayers! How one can ascend these rues? "A soul for a soul," *It* whispered. What beneficence of a trade this quote is could never fuze fragments to once join two souls. Unknown energy and time, contrived eons ago, a union fragmented and scattered in the vast void evermore. I ponder loudly—*It* heard my thoughts—home does

not shelter and glisten—with my love, Lucy Lenore.

Spawn of Cthulhu! This hollow man, this stuffed man, this fiend of night smiling; hell's grim visage not comforting this heavy pact, this chilling clime not encouraging me to act. Yet, *Its* hoary visage sent a killing sensation; and, it kept sinking and causing a hastening hallucination and linking this killing sensation to my diminished soul!

No more, said I, no more!

I could not torture my beloved back into this ghastly plane! Perhaps this trickster's illusion was my confusion. These whispers recede as I stood near the shore, ruminating on the night tide; felt Lenore by sea. *It* shall not free me as the moon's beam did not seem like a dream on this chilling winter's night. *It* will not gain what *It* coveted tonight:

I, and Lenore, "Nevermore!"

III

From this journey, onward back, toward her stone site in her native place of rest, and not trod loudly lest I disturb her dreamy rest! Amid trodden grounds endured from this quest, no foul scourge obstruct what sang of heart, no plight of devil's intent ever seed and dissever apart, no evil howls the luster on tonight's moon; soon unshackle

as I implore her name once more—nothing more!

Before I, embark unto my lovely Lucy's solemn place, I peer upon her grave; the grace beheld heaven's face, misplaced by night's terror, an upswing breeze sank with the might of hell's tide towards my Psyche, and did not salvage error from terror the bearer must face with Nike's blade. It lingers in whispers and whispers implore I— yes, I to my beloved by the shore and nothing more.

"Prophet!" said I, "if child of prophet!—foresee this fate!"—oh, father's endeavor was his sole aim, and dissever that once tether us never the same as it severed mother, mother fell lesser, lesser of things that grew in the nether, and the pleasure of kisses filled with terror—wrecked her, and tremors severed the sole treasure who gave heart measure—all this and nothing more.

This place, someplace, somewhere, something haunting this lot, eerie shadows overcasting their taunt: a tremble ripples in long-drawn-out sigh frozen in line. Behold, my dear, I have adored the intimacy spent here; oh—the torture of this terrible situation meant the unrest atoning in my shackles; and only the sainted maiden angels name Lenore—unshackle this stain and nothing more.

If I was prime to indulge in the fondest memories that won't fill me in rapturous pain or dare venture the languish I earn to gain in my stay, and this passion has led me astray as I take my last steps towards her stone site...once I took a sip of heaven's finest sanguine—how could I seek to vanquish the taint of history smear itself evermore...
     Yes, this I implore!

The mossy stone, a single lily foretold around surrounding violets... chilling ground chilled her lips; the chill knew no bound, stone casting frosty veil upon violets, moonlight embracing my lily shone cruelness choked in silence, sobbing eyes, pulsating sound of tides; here tears collecting above her abode, the chill still earth rang and swore—
     "she is here no more!""

And faith, never reassemble the bond that came undone, oh—heaven much farther than I thought, and it wanders aimless like a dark shooting star, awash by billions of stars on a black canvas, several too many light years apart. An overflow of ambivalence strains the unheroic heart, none seek out—the unhonorable heroic grave in these trample parts—never trampling, nevermore.

And the chill, never flitting; the killing chilling filling on the stone site betwixt her and me; If I had seen what's trapped inside bleeding walls, I would find solace in my lover's warm bed and not the lone, cold delusional despair. Quiet death laid here, my darling—my lovely darling Lily—my blushing bride, my wife, my life, the one and only Lucy, Lily Lenore—Won't be lifted—nevermore!

The Fifth

It was long, long ago foretold in Revelations
of an event where streams gushed down
and smashed into villages—and they say
nothing more than wild imaginations;
while smokey clouds followed without thought and the day
drenched by crooked rain as it struck down;
and these are the themes that live within omens.
And they now say the coming of the four horsemen.

The bull of war, the decrepit of famine,
The scourge of pestilence, the soulless death;
made no mention of the undiscovered ruins of the fifth
that's linked to the coming horrors of the Apocalypse.

Is it the reluctance of humans to deny the manifestation
that bears their sins and the unmentioned fifth
who rides in the shadow of the four not scribed in Revelations,
and only draws forth when Judgment Day is nigh—
and the turning of faith—surely in compassion
will surely cleanse the unbearable shame—
as they are shaken to say the coming of the fifth!

And it rode in with the darksign of humanity
long ago forgotten of yore bearing a stain
ring in fire and it will suffuse the torment
and Hatred's Will accompanies; it assures an ire
of the coming day and imprisons feeble souls that shall
cement the unwise counsel bellowing of weighty sins
under the mass hysteria and silent inaction
and the few who repent knew the root in Original Sin.

Madness infects and they scour in the name of Free Will,
unveiling the tragic beauty in the cruelty of living and with
that golden compass hoping will guide them on the long-unwinded

road filled with fog where the mind screams—in protest!
Against the Ill-Will wishing the lot of broken resolves—
too soon dissolve the last golden threads of heaven's
radiant light and it dims a chilling death and the fate
of one's bond is the sentence towards hell's domain
and the symbol of hope's light can't reach with its might
and what last remains upon this night the incarnation of the fifth.

The Lull of Laments

From the beginning of dreams of enchanted scenes
of sunrise kisses of no end nor of skyline nor filled on dead sea;
and lovers seem to carve their initials in the willow tree
and life, none taken, soon dislodged from their seat
of broken tempest and gaudy day denies a torrent scene.

We sought the ends of earth a sacred scene soon harrowed
by a dying, empty wasteland and drawing near the chill that filled
the air of stilled sorrows betrayed a higher power not shower
and cradle close towards vacant beliefs brewing an ill-power.

And scenes smolder the light of day, steering human's ways
and offerings could spoil and not tread close to darkness's strife
and tether a candle's fire and not succumb to the gluttons of life;
a pervading screech in these barely lit halls of sorrow
thought of beholding great blessings of adoring tomorrows.

And, finally, hail with adoring eyes lights the way and heeds words
of the crown head, detached not of love but of borrowed words,
and laid in its core foolish enough treading in hell's landscape.
Where once a delicate rose, plucked in the only chasm of light
and the surrounding darkness, drew the scorn of night's thorn
and, failing with obscure eyes, a rose with its thorn,
cut with its edge foreboding an insufferable hellscape.

The Mirror Resonance

What is that sound resonating in the halls of symmetry,
peering beyond in these halls of mirrors held in misery
and frames decorated with willows of my infidelity?

I cringed in fear, staring down the dimmed view
in the long stretch shadow of these vacant walls
dedicated in honor to the tribute that hid in each room.

One look I took, my pores seeming clogged, my sight blurred
at this mirror's distance and the misfortunate of it I must concur.
I fancy with this silly venture that spoke of something mental
with a second gaze from the corner made my heart tremble!

A sneer amid a dimly lit face petrified me in foreboding halls.
No hope assembling the chains that junction me to these walls
with mirrors of the third eye. I knew I had to face the thralls
of ones I dismissed, groveling shadows stretching unending halls.

The Spark in the Dark

Four seasons bear the dim spark its absence,
and marked tales read on the tapestry: men
deprived of their light; and yet they still thrive
in these inhospitable weathered nights,
and reminisce the gallant strides in lights
resolve, as they hope that they have arrived?

A rift gouged for miles and scar the lone world,
stood Fate on one side and Seren the other;
this crossroad was destined to sever
bonds and with haste sapped their vitality;
and barely grasping the commonality
of this grim picture and the sacrifice
one must give up—upholding the steep price
of this bond; as dimless light grew darker,
and stumbled in light's shadow and harbor
in that core a lifeless spark in the dark.

And in the core spoken by the Muses
hung the jaded figures with nature's clues:
revealed the cosmic forces resides a dark
art and scatter unto the whimpering
breath of Aether, and Nyx rode with the cloak
of Darkness and remnants of Hemera
fades in the eyes of men—dims the last spark.

The Uncheerful Cry

The smell of leather-laden towns ever pours down
the nostalgic scenes that held back unshaken frowns.
Reminisce: the tempestuous plunge of the depths
and the weight of shame unseeming staggered breaths.

And bear how—the stories that haunt the minds
and they ruminate over the harrowing night and find
deep in the gorge what sorrows are left behind.
soon hear its cry and ignore its uncheerful pain
and on this unordinary day what sane-praise
would raise its piercing cry of uncheerful cries?
Oh! foretold in omens of the avowal diminished souls
where hope's prayer would deliver salvation!
Unspoken truth would sooner crave in recreation—
and not bear the volatile witness of the upturned thread,
drenched in sins that could not kindly offer wine and bread.

Above the coils of passion a redeeming tale—ill-favored
by the sordid soil of its roots where faith wavered.
And with time all those crimes soon to be forgotten
and the prospect of tomorrows—of buried urns rotten,
lost in the landscapes of drear, while the entrapped souls
linger like wisp in the harrowing forest—eternal in throes.

Tides Ever Subside

When will the agony of my story end?
When will the tides ever subside?
Shall love ever defend or condescend
into a barren land that hides what died?
When will the agony of my story end?

When will the tides ever cascade aside
the unlikeness of sunny and moonlit skies?
As sea level rises, washing ashore a terrible raze,
and the howl brimming of the sunlight's pride,
and the glow dreaming from the moonlight's eyes
raising the torrent of tides that soon graze
the unsettled mind of cosmic horror, Typhon.
When will the crescent moon fade over the horizon?
When will this world cease with memory lane,
and take with it the shades of ash of those horrific days?
When will Spring flowers once again blossom in May?

When will the agony of my story end?
When will the tides ever subside?
Shall love ever defend or condescend
into a barren land that hides what died?
When will the agony of my story end?

Time Lapse

The cruel subtle collapse of the banal—rages
in wild flight and night kept in hidden pages;
a lapse in time that mangles unsaid words
once believed in; too soon erased towards
canals flowing of time and the same with all
onto living things with equal quiet fall;
and static photos never seem to fade,
in the distant cold death surely has made
and take back what is owed; and heaven's Lord
beckons with gilded eyes unsheathe the sword
could scarcely glaze and could never reign
our fears towards desolate hell's fiery plane.
And if Death knocks, welcome with blank resolve;
soon gone the loved ones and thee shall dissolve.

Tolling Bells

The bell tolls! Tolling sledging bells
from thy cradle to thy grave, the (upstart) clock foretells
the allotment of time and hear its somber horror
tick-tock, tick-tock, tick-tock;
how its measly ticks press the jubilant joys of terrors
and seconds go unhindered as tolling bells
lay in the hands of Moirae as they foretell
and pricks the mind in ticks, ticks, ticks,
and renew thyself in the sight of Sibyls
—in the twenty-four-hour swing of pendulums—
tick-tock, tick-tock, tick-tock—
reverberates in one's frantic mind upon the last hour!

The pendulum bird too soon at noon hour—
shrieks, shrieks with its foul coo!
and pay homage of its power
of that golden ball that hangs in grace and who
would raise alarm before nightfall welcomes Grim
with generous sounds of gothic bells—
ding dong, ding dong, ding dong,
alights the ravaging fire as God's hymn—
celebrate and siege with heart the long-
ing allotment of life and in passion's ring—hell
sings to the rhyming and the chiming of ringing bells.

Oh, the underbreath of chimes humming too loudly
along in the same stride—who knew
the pendulum bird jumps too soon at midnight hour—
shrieks, shrieks with its foul coo!
embrace the thralls of joys and sorrows—and proudly
ruminate of its stricken horrid power
of the bell tower—for the clock soon ceases
and straddles by these leases—and not find here the peace
upon the arrival of the midnight train how it clangs, and clashes,

74

and roars at once! Aboard each soul and carry in passage
bearing away from the golden gates of mighty heaven
and meander on these earthly fields with their havens;
and on their nights in the midst of their shadows the absence
of heaven's gleam: no glimmer of light is found as the death knell
signals and ingress night's terror stirring one's mind—as hell
sings to the rhyming and chiming of tolling bells—
dwells thy last hour dong, dong, dong with fright!

Have thy rest for the next passing—toiling bells
ring, ring, ring, in dark palls—before madness yells
where blessings laid in the dribs and drabs humming too loudly
with their oxidized bells—clang, clang, clang; and proudly
sung the melancholy testament of something serene, special
in the lowering of the brazen bell—howl its last chime
where tales of terror in their turbulency tells of the devil's
moans and groans of the bell tower keeper Poe's
creaking, squeaking, screeching the bell tower's rope
—toiling bells, bells, bells—unflinching time
rolling on the hills of hell,
the discord of Poe's tolling bells, bells, bells
—bells, bells, bells...

Unchosen Path

The closed-in lonely nights, all locked-up in the mind,
often held the shades lovers dare not tread to find.

Recall the scenes that linger in these musky woods
and hide amid caves and among shrubs of these woods.

And it held, the miasma of nightmare touched here
for those who passed their hikes often too near.

The haunting that kept this foreboding place its name
where balm not mend and wiser all the same
with lovers treading on lands of unholy soils
and hasten the rise of jaded shattered souls—
and tattered souls strewed about the song of their tolls.

If paired hikers chosen the unseeming path
and from that unassuming newfound bypath,
ventured away where ghosts do not linger;
would never stir the qualm of foul figures
lest their wrath and with nothing to forgive,
would not bar the very life they would live.

Undivine

Fear not, Lady Grace gilded in light,
what once chilled now met with divine,
sank low a warmth, radiating a shine;
somewhat saddened to find the sting of her blight.

I dwell in that encounter of Lady's blight
in delight of the calm, she exudes her sign
of that moment buzzing where her shine
went soaring, I couldn't stop thinking about the blight

I linger here, dazzled by this spectral sight
for a time an ash filled with a sign,
not of blue skies but of gloom that aligns
that night—I couldn't stop thinking about the blight.

The turn of hot summers chilled of the might
of heaven's blessing sent from a bloodline
in awe, only settled by the rapt benign
grace—I couldn't stop thinking about the blight.

The sunset in its strange gloom pours in night,
and the rise of a heavenly body enshrines
the husk of death of Lady undivine
grace—saddened to find the sting of her blight.

Unease of the Maiden's Name

In time, spark the flame of vengeance;
bode a troth forged in crime,
do not partake if lies should die
and wipe such vile scenes where
hearts weep—weep the unease of joys—
and the wanton plunge of that blunted blade,
instilled the coming of haunted ash nights;
forlorn by ghost wedge in the dreams
held this unchiseled blade;
dream provoking in equal turn,
she feigns hearing and bears
the plight of my shame did not sing
a song of succor, but of jarring chords
reverberating in these depthless walls.
They torture in the seams and screeches
and pierce with a pitch and scars the brow,
and it stretches with the length of the morrow
and bore a scene my eyes could not discern—
nor recall a time the soft threads of hers;
if she felt the weight of her words—
nor utter the words of the maiden's name.

Unholy Ghost

The trudge among this perpetual fog leads nowhere.
And what I left behind are diminished threads of yore.
The hollow air chokes with impunity as I tread
this ghastly realm that stalks my dreams and somewhere
in that once held enchanted scenes I could once
see with clarity, neither here nor there on the horizon.
Never fathomed the mist would shroud with such weight
and the desperate measure of it all could not wait!
Maybe the selfish relief under these invisible chains
could not resolve what swayed hope's gain in this foul turbulent wind.
Oh!—my soul's torch wanes by the gravity of this realm's foul mood.
The droplet of tears pocket my sight in swelling dunes
and the voice of courage—usurped by its horrid tune
laid the ruins of that once held the thriving gilded nation
their unshaken walls sturdy under siege. Tower of Babel,
collapsed under men's hubris: "come, let's create a name for ourselves
erecting a city and a tower whose top is in the heavens."
And not for this journey that led me here. Surely heaven's glow
shall invite in triumphant and cheer for the conviction of the soul.

I still yearn for a dream and not these nightmares under this fog
that schemes with its cruel siphon the unwavering strain and
where no plea is heard and my rapture only fed this horrid fog
and it drains the youth that it surely proved. And I recall all my sins
could surely prove my unwavering faith amid heaven's fading stars
—dimming the joys I held close in this deafening place's throng,
bear an essence filled the unfair the unseeming joys of songs
and the discord of its strum soon departs and scenes fold and shrink
in this choking cruel fog. The ash of its atmosphere soon forgets
why I wander here, strolling in this ungainly place with nothing
much in sight—and it's the perpetrator of my very plight!

Like a child unaware, the strange tales of terror I felt here that bought
my shaken thoughts as I fade with the ghastly fog—a nameless
vagrant splintered somewhere between these realms and in this fog's
fertile soil I wander in the silhouette of a ghost, a spirit of sins,
a shadow that embodies what I hid from most, I am drifting,
travailing the innermost chamber, the Unholy Ghost.

Veils of Sorrow

What is concealed inside are the veils of sorrow
and heaven's gift must reprieve the world of turmoil,
and not let the veils of sorrow flow into tomorrow.

The capsule of time soon narrows
the shroud of meaning and swiftly recoils:
what is concealed inside are the veils of sorrow.

Life like a tapestry written of heroes
whose might fought against demon's spoils
and not let the veils of sorrow flow into tomorrow.

The gleam filled with a mystery and harrowed:
something dark laden within did coil:
what is concealed inside are the veils of sorrow.

A lonesome spade in a game of faro
wishes to be availed in a deck of ace; foiled
and let the veils of sorrow flow into tomorrow.

In friendship find could never stray in sorrow
and return a comfort in the closing of breath nor toil
in assurance of cold trembles of the maidenless spoil;
what is concealed inside are the veils of sorrow.

Yoke of Fate

When tomorrow is near, where tomorrow is not quite far,
what of tomorrow brings us here, under the sea of stars.
Ah!—yesterdays, that time then, do you recall when yesterdays
are far behind—but distant now? What do I know of todays
when fond keepsakes lived in yesterdays and tomorrows anew;
and recall more than what devours tomorrow's joys and through
mountain peaks, we have not ascended to heaven's reach.

I mourn for today—we relent and give notice to yesterday,
which held fonder times and tomorrow new hopes; yet, today
creates those scenes with tomorrow's aspirations and dreams
seem all the same with fervent passion that heaven's beseech.

Is it not of sorrows we gave rise to capture joys in its many forms?
Is it not of tears we gave attention to the rising sun's warmth?
Is it not of fears where courage is found venturing the cold north?
Is it now for our suffering we search our meanings, thenceforth?
Is it not for these things that live in the yoke of fate of today?
What of yesterday and tomorrow brings us here to stay?

Life shoulders erecting from Earth's slumber an eternal rest
and here lies for us all—life and death in one's sobering quest.

Please Review This Book!

Reviews help authors more than you might think but also readers; it will help spread the word by reaching more readers who can glean value from this book and pass it on.
If you enjoyed *Shadows Amongst the Threads*, please consider leaving a review—it would be greatly appreciated—truly.

JASantana.me/ReviewShadows

Free Audiobook

DOWNLOAD THE FREE AUDIOBOOKS!

Grab your FREE audiobooks of *Shadows Amongst the Threads* and *The Cool and Warmth of Hearts,* narrated by me! Experience the chilling world of fear and the passionate realm of love in a whole new way.

JASantana.me/ShadowsHeartsAudio

DOWNLOAD THE FREE AUDIOBOOKS!

Grab your <u>FREE</u> audiobooks of
Shadows Amongst the Threads and
The Cool and Warmth of Hearts, narrated by me!

Experience the chilling world of fear and the
passionate realm of love in a whole new way.

JASantana.me/ShadowsHeartsAudio

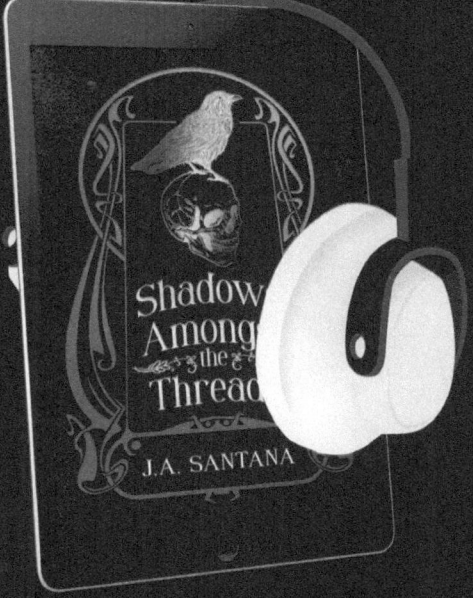

ABOUT THE AUTHOR

Driven by a passion for writing, Jose seeks greater wisdom to impart through his work. He craves new experiences, seeking to delight readers by transporting them to imaginative places through his writing.

He believes in using his stories to gain a deeper understanding of human nature and the human condition—including both the good and the bad within us. Jose is particularly interested in exploring the meaning of life, death, and what may exist beyond our realm. He aims specifically to discover insights to help people better navigate the world and the journey of life.

He draws inspiration from diverse sources such as mythology, history, psychology, philosophy, science, and his own keen observations. Through his poetry, Jose seeks to explore the darker aspects of human nature, encouraging readers to confront and integrate their own shadows. His collection, *Shadows Amongst the Threads*, embodies this journey into the gothic and the unknown.

Connect with Jose

jasantana.me

YouTube.com/@jasantana

jasantana.me/socials

More books coming soon.
You can sign up to get a sneak peek of the books I'm writing, notified of new releases, books I'm reading and recommend, giveaways and pre-release specials.

Acknowledgements

There are so many to thank and acknowledge who have influenced, inspired, mentored and/or supported me, this section would be quite longer than the actual book. With that said, I will do the best to make this thorough and concise.

Thank you to my parents, Francis, Agnes, and Jose Sr.; brother Andy; my child Tsunade; our cats Nature and Vincent; Uncles Juan, Alberto, Alex, Willy; Aunts Camille, Denise; my cousins Frankie & Erica, Will & Amanda, Jae & Crystal, Jessenia & Danny, Alexandra, and their children. Thank you to the rest of my family and those no longer with us (I miss you very much: grandpa, great-grandpa & great-grandma, Alexandra, and Blacky and Fluffy). Thank you to my closest friends Steve and Latonya. Thank you to the mother of my child, Linda, and her family. Thank you to the many friends and acquaintances I've known and gotten to know on my journey. Thank you to the artists, poets, authors, psychologists, philosophers, and to any that I miss. Thank you to nature and its splendors and thank you to the logos itself.

Thank you to my editor Michael Martin and my book cover & typeset designer Natalia Junqueira for their patience and professionalism in my book collaboration process.

Thank you, reader, for giving this book a chance and hope for the added value it has on your life, and it continues to do so as some source of wisdom and contemplation around the nuances of the shadow.

Thank you, writing community, for the invaluable wealth of knowledge in the production and marketing of a book; especially the overwhelming amount of information to run an author business.